HAPPY

Coloring Book

The Secret To Creating More Through Color

Created By Terry Robnett

Illustrated by Veronica Fernandes

Published by Liberto Press

Castle Rock, Colorado, USA

ISBN: 978-0-9974466-2-3

www.LoveHealingBalance.com

www.Facebook.com/Lovehealingbalance

Getting Started On Your Journey

The secret to creating more through color is based on the concepts used in the law of attraction combined with the effects of color on the human mind. According to the law of attraction, we bring things we desire into existence and attract through our thoughts and feelings. The belief is that we create what we think about most.

You chose this book for a reason. While you are coloring, make sure that your thoughts and attention are genuine and blissfully on **HAPPY**. Notice what that looks like for you. Each page has an illustration of a symbol that represents **HAPPY**. This helps you to focus on detail while engaging in enjoyable creative coloring.

In the process of creating **HAPPY** through the law of attraction, it is absolutely necessary to apply positive thinking. Creating more through color is intended to be an enjoyable, fun and stress free activity. So sit back and relax your mind and body. Doing this is known to increase brain power. Don't you want more of that?

Pick a page that really jumps out at you! Seriously, you can start anywhere in this book. Be sure that you are really interested and excited about the page you are coloring. Keep your mind open to the creative energy you are putting into your masterpiece. As you color each page, your focus is now on the image that represents **HAPPY**. Your thoughts now become more positive, expansive, and creative. You won't even realize it but while you are engrossed in your coloring, your emotions will become happy, proud, and excited. These are only a few of the thoughts, feelings and emotions that have been experienced by many others while using this book.

After you are done coloring (whether it is finished or not), go to the back blank lined pages of the book. Now that you have had a chance to expand your mind and increase your brain power, you will use these pages to express your gratitude by writing "I am so excited and grateful now that I am **HAPPY**". Close your eyes, take a deep breath and visualize what **HAPPY** looks like for you in your mind's eye. Make mental note of every detail of that image in your mind and hang on to that crystal clear vision so you can think about it several times a day. The most important part of the law of attraction is to feel as if you already have it. How does it make you feel to HAVE and BE **HAPPY**? It is important to act, speak and think as if you are genuinely **HAPPY** right now. After you open your eyes and now have a GREAT BIG smile on your face, feel free to write down all of the other things you are grateful for. Be patient and know that you are deserving. Keep your thoughts positive and always remember, "*Happy* is as simple as a choice"!

For more books & life enhancing info go to: www.LoveHealingBalance.com

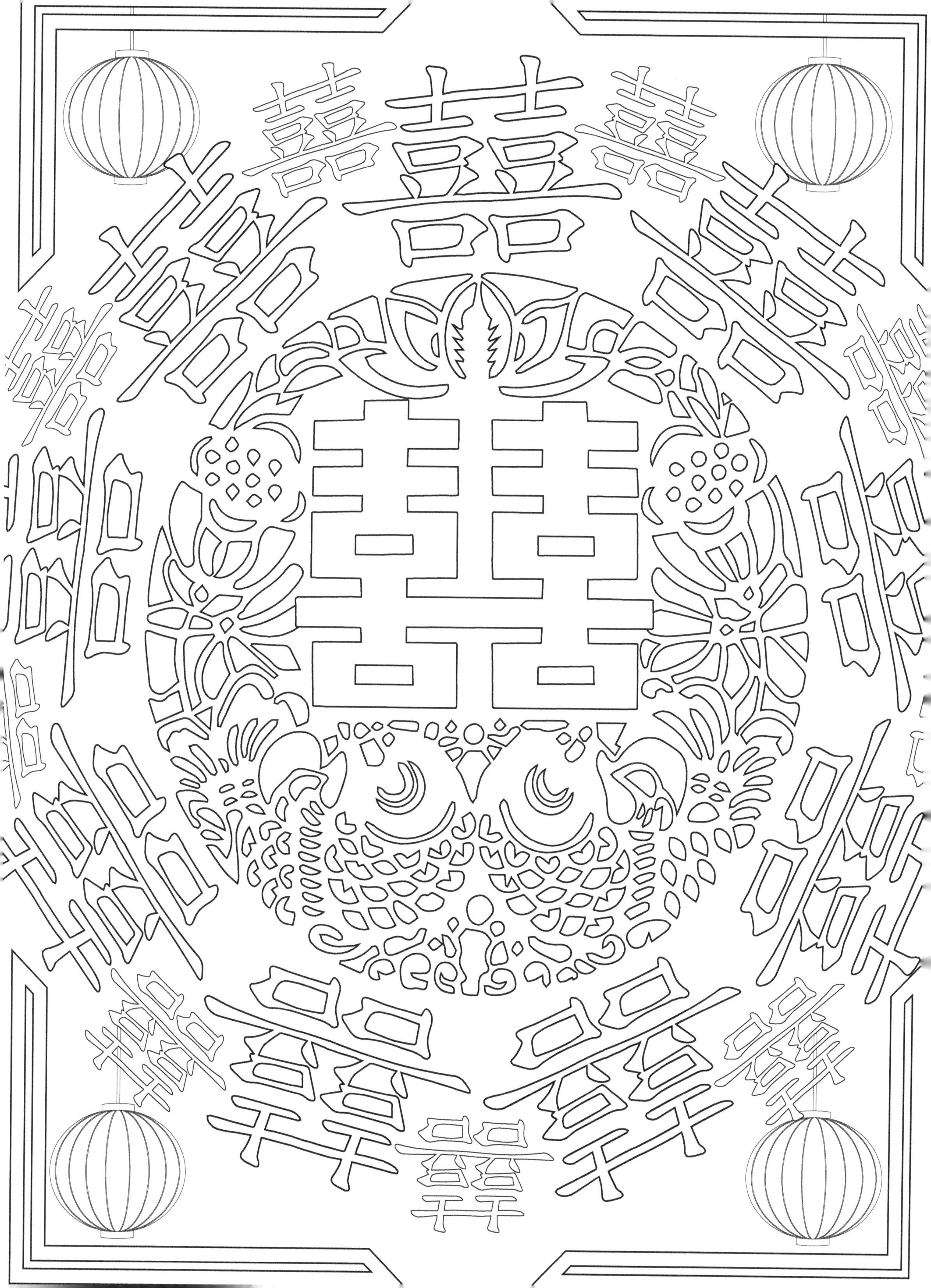
囍

Hakuna Matata

HAPPINESS

Happy As a Pig In Mud

HAPPINESS

HAPPINESS

HAPPINESS

HAPPINESS

HAPPINESS

HAPPY

Laugh

Grin

HAPPY

HAPPY

Giggle

Smile

HAPPY

I am so excited and grateful now that I am HAPPY!

ABOUT THE CREATOR

Terry Robnett lives in California with her husband and 3 children. She thrives on her purpose as an intuitive leader poised like the beacon of light that inspires many. Terry does this all with a mission of creating a global environment that promotes love, healing and balance. She lives each moment smiling and happy as she pursues her passion as a motivating mentor helping and teaching people to make positive shifts in their life.

It is through Terry's purpose and passion that the series of Coloring books "The Secret to Creating More Through Color" was actualized. The whole idea is to open your eyes to a world of endless opportunities! Creating more through color engages you in the concept used in the law of attraction. This is the ability to actualize whatever you are focusing on into your life by using the power of the mind to convert whatever is in your thoughts and materialize them into reality. Regardless of gender, age, nationality or religious belief, this resourcefulness is available to ALL of us. Life is a blank canvas of possibilities where you are in control, so why not relax and have fun doing it by creating more through color?

Visit Terry's website to see more books and to sign up for FREE Daily Pumps guaranteed to uplift and make you smile: **www.LoveHealingBalance.com**